Rewriting Human Narrative

One heartbeat at a time!

Surendra Soni

To

The Supreme Creatrix,

the Divine Mother,

for being the eternal source of energy and

inspiration.

To

Late Mrs. Vimala Gupta

And

Late Dr. G. P. Gupta

For introducing me to the writings of

Sri Aurobindo and the Mother.

To

The great teachers

who have guided and shaped me.

To

My academic mentor,

Late Prof. B. G. Tandon

And to

My beloved wife,
Tanujaji,

and my sons,
Auro
&
Aatmaj,

And
my extended family and cherished friends,

for their unwavering love, warmth, and support!

Acknowledgement

At the outset, I wish to express my heartfelt gratitude to the great teachers who nurtured my love for language and literature.

At higher secondary level, I had the privilege of learning English grammar from an exceptional teacher, Shri Ramesh Dikshit. I take great pride in the fact that, though he has superannuated officially long ago, he has since embraced the nobler role of an author, enriching the world with his insightful books on the religious and cultural heritage of the great city of Ujjain. Even as an octogenarian, he has been serving the society with great energy and fervour. Not only his students, like myself, but the larger society feel grateful to him and cherish him and his services as their invaluable treasure.

At college level during my graduation, I got the opportunity to learn English literature from a great teacher, Professor F. A. Jilani.

Despite his administrative duties as the Principal of the College, he spared his personal time to guide me. Though he is not physically with us today he resides in the hearts of his students like me forever.

At university level, I got the opportunity to learn, and receive personal guidance, from great teachers like Prof. K. K. Kemkar, Prof. D. S. Tatke and Prof. Ms. Nirmaljeet Oberoi to whom I shall remain forever grateful. Although they are no longer with us in body, their spirit and influence endure, residing in the knowledge, values, and lessons they imparted, which continue to guide and inspire us.

My alma mater, Vikram University, Ujjain and especially the Department of English where I studied as well as served as a teacher would always enjoy a place of pride as a distinguished institution in my heart. So would the Govt. Degree College and Yashwant Higher Secondary School, Mahidpur.

I feel grateful to BookLeaf Publishing and their team whose help and support saw me through at every stage of the writing and publication of this book.

Preface

As a student of English literature, the taste I cultivated for great poetry goes very deep as a background to this book of poetry.

But even much deeper goes the influence of the teachers who taught me language and literature. They wove the magic of language and literature in my teenage and early twenties' psyche.

Combined with some glimpses of life and nature, it's this magic that flows through these poems.

Often, my psyche struggles to overcome the impression of anything cruel taking place in society or whatever defies peace on my mind and consciousness. Needless to say it tends to find expression in these poetic outpourings.

One of the poems in this collection claims we can heal the ills and evils of our society and rewrite the human narrative one heartbeat at a time replete with unconditional goodwill, love and compassion. I feel many poems tend to add to this feel in this collection and impart the book with its title. If this feeling gets communicated to the reader, this book would have achieved its goal.

Students looked up to her!

Students looked up to her!
Every gesture of hers counted!
Her gaze pierced deep into their being!
Her words moved their minds,
Her voice stirred their hearts!

Every day, she took great care,
To weave her words into
A delicate chain of clear thoughts!

Every day, she took pains
To get straight to the core
Of young minds!

Everyday she poured her heart
Into the young hearts
Listening to her with rapt intent!

She knew their roots
Must be firmed up
In a well-cultivated soil of values!

She knew their minds
Must be refined,
Never to gather the dirt of dogma!

She knew their hearts
Had to be so sensitized,
Never to dry up
From the calming succulence of compassion!

She knew it was necessary
To keep humanity alive
Into the ever-growing bulge of populace!

I am fascinated by a boy!

I am fascinated by a boy
Who cannot speak,
Nor can he listen!
But he has something in him
That makes one wonder
Even leaves them stunned!

It's a sight to watch him shoot
A target ten meters apart!
With his hand rock stable,
He can aim and shoot a dot.

Nothing deters him,
He commands his breath.
No thoughts disturb him,
He commands his mind!

Shot after shot,
He shoots with finesse!
Without a word uttered or heard,
He stands out in the worldly race!

A small canteen

A small canteen,
Yet occupying business!
Its young owner and his wife,
With four of their kids!

They run it all day long,
While the kids play along,
Riding their baby scooter,
Or dancing to the tune of some song!

Apparently, there is nothing wrong!

Some customers go in for tea,
Some for snacks, many for both.
A shelf-full of cigarette packets,
With most customers opting to smoke!

The kids are free to eat and drink!
All is free for them all day round!
Tea, soft drinks, junk food,
And the floating clouds of smoke
Drifting overhead all day around!

Within me lay!

Within me lay
An oceanful of night, and,
An oceanful of day!
But who speaks from within,
And to whom does it say
These mighty thoughts
Welling up from human clay?

Vast expanses are felt,
And profound depths embraced,
All packed in this fragile shell,
With I, Me, My stamped in place!

Then this web of brain,
With its intricate neuronal train,
All caught in complexity—
A swelling ego, and its inflated claim,
Managing all with its dexterity!

A small object

A small object serves us long!
Years and years, it tags along!
As we use it something gets stuck,
It's cleaned up, and nothing goes wrong!

A piece from our kitchen utensils,
For example—
We cook or serve our food in,
Day in, day out!

They stay with us,
Sometimes a lifetime.
We treat them as lifeless—
But aren't we rather stony
Just if we care to look inside, in case!

Is it just a matter of attitude?
Or of growth?
Either we stay insensible, or,
Grow in kindness and gratitude!

Diwali celebrations

Diwali celebrations,
A cacophony of firecrackers!
All types of sounds
they produce!

Thud, boom, rumble;
crack, pop, whistle!
Chirp, sizzle, zip;
Rat-a-tat, boom-boom, tick-tick!

Then come, there the special effects,
crescendo and finale!

Tourbillon, dragon's roar, whirlybird;
building boom, echoing fade, climactic burst!

Just a few things are missed,
As they often are.
Sparrow's cheerful chirp,
Robin's whistled songs,
Mynah's rich, throaty calls,
and hornbill's low and gruff!

Parakeet's high-pitched chattering,
Drongo's rich musical notes,
Owl's hooting low-pitched calls,
and nightingale's melodious flute-like songs!

We celebrate with firecrackers,
Just unmindful or least aware
That we disturb, disrupt, and damage,
The life of our feathered friends!

World Peace

Right since my childhood days,
I have heard or read,
With unwavering grace,
Nothing more important than this—
And that is world peace!

Half a century has elapsed!
The subject remains ever fresh!

With slight alterations made,

The waters remain as troubled as ever to
wade!

Let's prepare notes on the issues
For our children, grand, great grand and so
on
And let our 'knowledge and 'wisdom' pass
on—
What we have studied with great resolve,
Yet never been able to solve!

A child and her innocence

A child and her innocence
Can win over even a cruel heart!
That's what sets humans apart!

When a child gives you a smile,
Can it ever fail to move you for a while?

When the little one's intelligence sparks,
It may just bring you pleasant shocks!

They apply their minds in innovative ways,
The elderly may not fathom the source of the
rays!

Wish to see an inside view of
the beauty of their hearts and brains?
Go explore nature's variety of
the beauty of blooms,
immense and intricate!

I was sober, he was drunk!

I was sober, he was drunk!

I was already seated well.
He came and took the seat beside me.

I was in my senses, but he wasn't!

I decided to move to another seat.
Got up and moved to the rear.
The bus started to move.

Tried my best to steer clear,
Yet lost my balance,
almost stumbled upon him.

He didn't say a single word.
I was sober, he was drunk!

Don't be just matter of fact!

A tree sprinkles its flowers upon the earth,
We trample upon them!

One would say, "They simply fall;
To walk upon them is nothing wrong!"

And what else would you do,
If no space is left to walk through!

Flowers bloom, they fall—
It's nature's rhythm, after all !

But just think, my dear friend,
A flower manifests nature's grace!

Pause for a moment, contemplate!
Nature's bounty transcends the material race!

Offer back, at least, feelings of love and
gratitude!!
Don't be just matter of fact!

I read the story of a queen!

I read the story of a queen,
She hailed from a modest background;
Greatness was woven into her being,
She lived and breathed
Values profound.

Piety was etched into her soul,
Compassion, integral to her character.
Valour came naturally to her—
Against the unjust she could act severe!

It's not my pursuit
To study her life
As a relic of an era, bygone!
I aspire, and feel sure,
They have sown seeds of greatness,
By those lived, not just for themselves,
But to leave behind
As a legacy to be grown.

I see great women around,
Who rule in their own sphere—
They have the courage to dare,
And the kindness to care.
Heroines in their own right,
Queens of resilience and might,
Fighting for causes, burning bright!

A father-daughter duo!

A father and a daughter—
Is a miraculous proposition!
Together, they have created wonders,
For when they join forces to achieve an aim,
Even gods find it difficult to check them,
From bringing dreams to fruition!

There are father-daughter duos
Whom it's a marvel to watch!
They work with missionary zeal
When together, they undertake a cause!

Their souls and minds so wonderfully align
Their energies work in complete harmony
Leaving no room for forces unholy,
No space for anything malign!

What do we buy a car for?

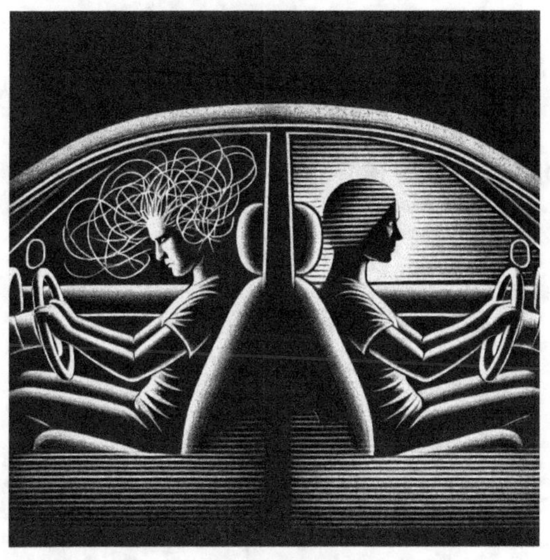

I wonder—what do we buy a car for?
Is it just convenience and comfort?
But quite surreptitiously,
Status and luxury tap us quietly on the back!
They have the power to suspend
Our power of discretion,
Which at times they can easily hack!
As soon as we cross
What feels like the affordability mark,
We tend to move under shadows dark!

Luxury and status have other ways to hold us
in domination
The best way to do that
Is to forward a better safety proposition!
But I again wonder—
What offers a greater certainty of protection?
A mind well under control and in balance
Or a car with more safety features and
airbags?

Existence and human mind

Every day, a new sun rises,
The existence is novel every moment,
A river renews itself as it flows!

Every day, the human mind extrapolates,
It adds to its burdens some new torment,
It gathers more dust as it goes!

We learn little from existence,
Though we are part of it.
We rarely discover what true love is,
Or how it interwines with compassion.
By any measure, we always fall short of it!

What's religion?

Does religion remain still alive,
If love and compassion for fellow humans die?

Does religion still throb
If helpless people are killed in its name
And their near and dear ones are mercilessly left
to sob?

Does religion still grow
If we water its roots
With malice and hatred
Put aside all fellow-feeling
And seeds of conflict sow?

What lies at religion's core
If global well being is not its concern
And human pain doesn't make it feel sore?

What's religion
If it's not the soul of humanity
How can it flourish
If it doesn't feed on
Compassion and charity?

What's religion
If it doesn't connect
One life with another
And within a single one
The heart with the head?

Rewriting the human narrative!

Often I think and meditate,
And let my understanding go
As far as it flows!

How can we bring to an end
All human pain and suffering,
All the torment and woes?

All that fuels wars and conflicts—
fanaticism, hatred, or malice,
whatever the seeds thereof sows!

If only we could learn,
Not just the maths of mind and memory,
But the poetry of the heart too—
How to resolve the sum of all,
And refresh ourselves all anew!

Love and compassion
Lose their meaning
If they can't undo
The harvest of the mind's design—
To rewrite the human narrative,
Altogether afresh other than how it goes!

So much noise!

So much noise within!
So much noise around!
Can they cancel each other out?

I took a deep plunge inside!
To launch on a search far and wide!

I was firm and determined
To leave no room, no space,
For the culprit to hide!

There is something that rises and falls,
There is inside oneself an ebb and tide!
There is something within that goes on a ride!

O my good lord!
Is it the I, Me, My and Mine of Myself,
And You, Your, and Yours of Yourself,
And all that we sum up as Other and
Otherself?

It's a horny race and ride
That we all tend to undertake,
Every now and then we raise our stake
And make a claim!

At every step, we compete,
We clap a flap on someone's light.
And take any hasty course
To beat others and brutally outvie

We have no time to light up
A pure flame inside
That emanates true light
And can make us genuinely outshine!
A restless, agitated course we prefer

Our peace we undermine!

That's what gives rise to so much noise
What you feel out and over there
Wells up first from within,
And spills from inside!

Mother Earth

The air is humid
And leaves me restless.
Yet the trees by the roadside
Propel me to keep my pace;
And the earth beneath my feet,
Keeps me firm-footed,
And prompts me to proceed,
As it slips back, step by step.

I don't say it's all in vain,
Seeds are sown and crops are grown
It all aligns, it all sustains.

But much of universe is a mystery,
As the life around and within me!
So many creatures are just born and get
killed!
Humans feel they're smart and can dominate
the whole scene!
But when earth alters its mood, and,
When the climate gets harsh and crude,
The air around, the trees beside, the earth
beneath and the clouds hanging high,
All get school-masterly
And teach humans a lesson
Keep within your limits
How dare you master Mother Mason!

A bundle of nervous energy!

A bundle of nervous energy,
She twists and turns!
In many a style she walks
In many a mood she runs!

Sometimes her hair flows free,
Vying with winds and leaves of a tree.
Often they are tied in tails curly,
Rarely are they woven well in buns!

In colourful apparel,
She looks so beautiful,
Her fingers are so nimble,
Her feet ever so swift.
One moment so agile,
Just another so cool!

She seems purely a nature's wonder!
For society she is just a preschooler!

A puff of cigarette!

I just wonder what they seek
In a puff of cigarette!
Then puff after puff,
They lose their vital energies,
Trying to exhale their worries,
They claim life is tough!

True it is,
There are phases in life
Smooth and rough.

But tell me, friend,
Why to take a dose
of drugs and smoke
When nature offers us
Calm of mind and heart's repose!

Then there are other things too
To indulge and practice
To build up positivity in life
And one's energies uplift!

Sports is one,
Such a fantastic activity,
Heavenly joy it can create,
And do away with all reactivity!

Meditation is another,
Which helps us discover,
Our true self and powers
It unplugs us and helps rise
Does away with all negativity
And makes us truly wise!

You might say
I sermonize!

But I ask
If life offers
A surer chance to win,
Why prefer to play dice?

I asked the thoughts to stop!

I asked the thoughts to stop, and,
Let me feel the morning breeze!
When nature (around) offers its bounty,
Why to let thoughts your mind seize!

Thoughts at times overpower,
Tend to arrest your breath
Nature tries to shake you free
Out of the inner tempest!

Feelings rejuvenate their power
When nature gives them a shower
Thoughts regain true power too
As nature bids them refresh anew

Nature in its varied beauty revels
Celebrates its colours, and,
Scintillates in its scents

So does it teach us
In our imagination to soar,
In feelings to enrich, and,
In thoughts to grow, and,
Flow in multifacets!

Why so much hue and cry?

Why so much hue and cry
As they return in iron chains
With their whole being shaken, and, their
consciousness,
All soaked in tear and sigh!

It is a 'lawful' transaction
All upto you, if you dub it inhuman
Between a nation
'Reclaiming greatness'
And another, 'once and forever, great!'

From one, humans flee
To fulfill their dreams
To the other
Who shows the iron will
To put them to the crushing mill
Wind up their aspirations
And put them under an iron seal
And flies them back like brute
Treating them not like
Humans with flesh and blood
But lifeless bags of jute!

This is how
Two 'great nations' decide,
How illegal immigrants
Would be brought to their knees!
Even if the soul of justice suffocates
And from the body of law flees!

Those forty hours!

Those forty hours
Felt to them like forty centuries!
Each second had borne
The burden of the dreams and aspirations
That at one stroke
Were set on fire
And burnt to ashes!

The golden gates they had once beheld,
Glistening with promise in the distant land,
Now stood as cold iron bars—
A cage forged from their own yearning.

Their hands, bound in rusted chains,
Held nothing but the weight of exile,
Their feet, shackled, traced the path
Back to the dust they had tried to escape.

The sky they had dreamed beneath
Now bore the silent witness
To their shattered hopes,
As they crossed the border,
Not as seekers,
But as shadows cast away.

The land of riches whispered no farewell,
Only the echoes of doors slammed shut,
Leaving them with nothing but
The bitter taste of what could have been!

One heartbeat at a time!

They picked issues,
They locked horns!
They could have sown
Seeds of flowers,
But they chose thorns!

A gesture of warmth,
A sweet smile, a kind glance,
A bit of compassion,
And a little patience—
Were the only heartfelt urge!

Instead, dislikes piled up,
Malice thrived,

Hatred grew,
Disrespect and scorn
Surged and multiplied!

As we live side by side as neighbours,
Could we grant ourselves some grace?
Not for the other's sake,
But for the cause of peace!

Just think of the old ones and the frail,
Just think of the little ones—
Putting aside only for a short while
The humdrum of life
Taking a corner seat!
Can't we change the course of life
One positive feel a moment,
At a time just one heartbeat?

Nature's magic overwhelms!

A cool breeze, a warm sun,
In the midst of a vast green land,
Jaggery churning out every few hours by the ton
In a hot boiling pan!

Ishwarilal, literally a son of God,
Constantly on his toes, turning a rod,
Making pure jaggery for half a century!

It is his religion, it is his yoga,
To serve nature's pure sweet,
To people from far and wide,
Who intermittently drive in!

Throw a glance around,
Wonderful people are found!
They are one with nature and God,
So innocently pure, so devoid of fraud!

They incessantly work,
Seek some help from bullocks,
At times replace them with
Their own shoulders,
To pull heavy loads
Of stubble and rind!

Nature's magic overwhelms,
Its sweetness it offers,
In its bounty, it serves.
Do we give it enough back,
Or just contrive to extract
As much as we can,
And stay restless, thinking
How little we're able to take?

The temple of justice!

The judge sat in his chair,
A class apart.
All others looked up to him,
And justice they sought.

Matters and issues
Were raised before him,
Which the judge
Tried hard to resolve.
Acts of law were referred to,
To take a clear call!

The lawyers took sides,
To help their clients win.
The state and its law
Loomed large,
Yet remained nowhere clearly seen!

Human nature, in its varied world
With all its tendencies
And complications,
present themselves

But do our judges know
What true dispassion is?
Can they see without bias
What pure observation ought to be?

If a judge sits over there,
Inobservant of human nature
As it plays out in those seeking justice, and,
As it plays out in themselves
Pleading for and delivering it!

If dispassionate observation,
Unbiased, detached, and pure,
Doesn't find space to enter
It's no longer
A temple of justice,
But merely a polished veneer!

They say age is just a number!

They say age is just a number!
Behind the age is the mindset!
A positive mindset helps a lot,
Yet most, in nature's web, get caught!

Mindsets don't suddenly rise!
The paths that we've treaded all life,
Get etched on our brains by and by,
Minds get set over course of time
Habits get built up, brains get conditioned.
That's how mindsets emerge!

Yet there's something deeper,
That we haven't yet been able to trace.
Somewhere deep the source of breath lies,
There's some profound base—
from where breaths arise!

If aging is not just a number,
Nor is it just a mindset!
Probably life energies have a much deeper origin,
They seem to be wedded with the seat of the self,
That lies far too deep within!

So it won't merely do to change the mindset;
Let us set out to trace the source of the self
But how could I tell more,
I'm a preschooler too, just an aspiring student!

What they are, they are!

What they are,
They remain.
What I am,
I sustain!

Beyond this dichotomy,
Beyond these parallel lines
Which cannot meet,
Exists the essence of 'what is'!

'What is' is not
What 'has been!'
Every moment, it's new—

It's beyond time,
And yet exists,
So you cannot weave it,
In a story
Or in a tapestry, sew!

It's not something
To please your mind with,
It's not something
You can apply your mind to!

Nor is it something
To ruminate on
Not even something
To rue!

Just a passing glimpse,
Nature offers us
Should we dare to perceive!
If one could distinguish
A drop of water on a floor
Or on a flower
A drop of dew!

One leaves a mark behind,
The other, dissolves without a clue!

City's busiest square!

This is the city's busiest square!
You might wonder—why should one care?
There's a school nearby!
You didn't ask as quickly, it matters why?
Every morning, on a working day,
There's a rush of life and vehicles every way!
People able-bodied and fragile
Push through every while!
Among the fragile, the weakest ones
Jostle ahead to raise their stake,
To prove their worth, to carve a name!
Among them proceed, an old lady and a kid,
Supporting each other, hand in hand;

In every young gentleman around,
The old lady looks for her son and the kid her dad!
Few feel for them, few proceed with due sense!

From nature to the divine!

Each flower so vivid,
Each leaf so lush!
Each branch a fragrant bouquet,
Each tree an offering,
From nature
To the Divine!

Each color so vibrant,
Each shade so rich!
Each spectrum a bouquet
Each spectacle an offering

From nature
To the Divine!

Each sound so vibrant,
Each frequency so rich!
Each symphony a bouquet,
Each orchestra an offering,
From nature
To the Divine!

Each breeze so rich,
Each wind so vibrant!
Each eddy a bouquet,
Each gale an offering,
From Nature
To the Divine!

Each stream so rich,
Each fountain so vibrant!
Each confluence a bouquet
Each sea an offering
From Nature
To the Divine!

His eyes were filled with wonder!

His eyes were filled with wonder,
Innocence etched deep into his face.
When innocence is wedded to wonder,
It's sheer amazement incarnate!

The little boy held a book close to his heart,
He knew not how to read,
And yet there was affinity of some sort,
He seemed to be knowing intuitively a lot!

Intuition and innocence go hand in hand,
The heart in its directness,
May have the perception of truth,
Which it may through the wonderment in eyes
flash!

The little boy himself symbolizes
A universe full of amazing spectacles
In his curly hair he holds its complexity,
In his large bright pupils its splendid wonders!

A child's innocence is a unique thing!

A child's innocence is a rare, wondrous thing!
Not something static, but has its own dynamics!

Just as in the morning, birds' voices to the heavens ascend,
Or as every morning from celestial heights sun rays descend,
Or the pure waters from the mountains fall,
Or somewhere from afar a flute gives someone a sweet call!

If you look into it deep within,
It gradually unravels a marvelous scene!
Fragrance of flowers is inherently ingrained,
The beautiful colors of nature find a fine blend!

If it breaks into its characteristic smile,
Its parallel is quite rare to find!
If it chooses to break into tears,
It holds the power to send your heart into shreds!

If it chooses to quietly interact,
It acts as a lever for heavenly transport,
But try to give it a word,
The whole range of human vocab would find it
difficult,
To convey its import!

Each time I set out to write a poem

Each time I set out to write a poem,
Every character stakes its claim!
A comma, at times, sends me into a coma,
A period doesn't halt the poetic force—
Often, it builds momentum and flings opens new
floodgates!

Every space, I tell you, carries its own life!
Just as every step imprints upon the earth,
Setting the pace of your movement,
As every breath weaves the rhythm of life,
And every breathless moment makes you realize
its dearth!

I said, 'every character'. Hold onto that!
Now—just take inverted commas.
They possess the power to enact a whole drama!

There are many more that go unmentioned,
Each one of them enjoys their own unique worth!

The heart does not beat in itself!

The heart does not beat alone,
It beats throughout the body.
You can feel its rhythm, its reverberations—
whether it's in balance and harmony!

The heart connects the soul with the mind and
the brain!
It is far more than just an organ,
In moments of deep meditation,
You can clearly feel,
It's an occult junction!

It responds to both the mind, its agitations
As well as to the self and its intuitions.
It's not merely a blood pumping station,
But a highly advanced center of communication!

A tribute to my English teacher

He taught us the difference
Between mediocrity and excellence!

While all teachers
Do a great job,
As they teach and train
In the fundamentals of a subject and its advanced
terrain

Great teachers go one step ahead.
They teach
not just facts and information,
But how to organize,
How truly to grow in knowledge,
And how to acquire
The essential wisdom
Of a subject and with it,
To soar into uncharted territories!

As a teacher of language
He taught us
Not just its grammar and syntax,
But how great minds use them to express
The very fabric of human thought
And the essential nature
Of the feelings and emotions within human heart!

A godly lordly cluster!

When the little child walks,
Divinity shines through its short steps.
Melodies break through
As it cries and babbles!

Such was the case with the little boy,
Who knew not what it meant to be shy!
He walked bare-bodied, as pure innocence does.
He seemed to be part of nature,
In all its beauties, colors and lustre!

As the boy joined a few more of same sort
Closing in on the bathtub
In the warm ambience of child's care,
giving one another a sweet rub,
Fairies jostled to give them a bath—
It was such a godly lordly cluster!

A glance at my watch

I took a glance at the time on my watch.
It set me thinking—
Deeply and for long!

So much work to be done,
So little time left.
If I could just put aside all anxiety
And take a plunge into the timeless!

But I didn't want to lose myself
Into some world abstract,
While my work stood still,
Paused and at rest,

And I feel elated,
As I sit aside and meditate!

If Arjuna could take a plunge
Into the Divine Song's eternal message
Amidst the battlefield,
And its surrounding challenge—

Then my work is no big deal.
I could as well take on a challenge
As I meditate on the self
Without letting my mind
Under anxiety reel!

As I meditated on the self,
The mind found it difficult to get anxious.
It was as if without a connect
Between the mind and the self,
The mind and anxiety got into a nexus!

As the mind worked
In the illumination of the self,
It found access to
Hidden treasures and wealth!
Not an ounce of work
Did I cast away
As underneath the vessel of the mind
I discovered

An ocean brimming with untapped potential!

Let the heart speak directly to the heart!

I thought a critical comment
Might serve the cause
Instead of
A positive heartthrob!

A sea of difference
I sensed in a while
All that could have gone straight, easily connect
Could have carried,
Much greater weight—

Yet in no time,

Lost its straightforwardness
Deformed into a convoluted shape,
Turned into
An unworkable mess!

We must learn the art—
When the heart could speak directly to the heart
Without allowing
The mind to intervene,
To distort a spontaneous creation
And thrust out an ugly scene!

Would we still fight?

If we truly loved
The mysteries of the universe
Would we ever fight?

Just take a deep plunge
Into the skies, stars, and their spectacles.
Aren't they enough to set us free
From our prejudices and their shackles?

All human knowledge,
Vision, and wisdom,
With all the paraphernalia of science and
technology

And their conundrum,
All quite genuine in their own right,
Fall miserably short to fathom their miracles and
might!

Don't they make us realize
How small we are and how ignorant too;
Would the universe's unresolved immensities ever
open our sight?

If we could delve deep
And dwell long enough
On universe's unexplored potential and
possibilities
To measure up to its real depth and its real
heights,
Would we still choose to fight?

Heartbeats

Does the heart beat the same
When you're quiet or in some game?

Does the heart beat the same
When you rise in love or sink into hate?

Don't heartbeats record how you feel,
Leading life straight or making some deal?

Does the heart beat the same
When you tend to get jealous,
When you feel moved to compassion,
Or inclined to get callous?

The heartbeats reflect both—
The mind that gives it twist,
And the conscience that gives it pricks!

Only the soul within
Can unshackle it of its burden!
It needs the light, purity,
and the sense of knowing
That all that's heavy or dark can enlighten!

As one is out for a ride!

As one sets out for a ride—
In a car or a bike,
On a bicycle or a scooter,
Straight as an athlete,
Or stylish as a cutie

Does one ever give it a thought,
Moving on a wide road
Or in a narrow street caught,
common space we share
common space is sought!

Why do we get rowdy on the road,
Speed becomes our goddess,

'I care not' our dominant mode!

Do we move out from our homes
As well-meaning Samaritans,
Or as a scoundrel freely roam?
If good will for all in movement around
Is not our orientation,
Are we collectively humane, in harmony and
sound?

A few moments of total peace

Does even the night
Instill in us
For just a few moments,
At least—
The habit to be totally quiet?

The humdrum of life,
So deep,
Gets settled
While the mind,
Round the clock,
Stays rattled!

A few moments
Of absolute peace—
Not to be mixed with
The habit to get exhausted
And then fall asleep!

Just a few moments
When nothing stirs,
Nothing makes us stir
Can do miracles,
Can help us access
The elixir!

Life's beauty lies in its hidden treasures!

Life's beauty lies in its concealed treasures!
Rarely do we work hard enough to have them
unearthed!
We stay content with whatever we inherit,
We're nothing more than just dowagers!

What lies on the surface for all—
To see, appreciate and wonder at
Is not the whole of it,
But just an ounce of the real secret!

Not that I claim to be a wiser one,
And seen it inside out,
I have only sought to peer
Deep into the self and its source.
There are seers who teach us the course,
It's their grace indeed,
Which helps us trace our real whereabouts
It's their light indeed,
Which leaves nothing to darkness and doubts!

The sannyasi facing his passions!

The *sannyasi* sat in a park,
To meditate deep and long,
To contemplate on what had gone,
So clearly awry, so utterly wrong!

He had relinquished
All his material possessions,
Yet there stood,
In rebellious defiance,
Raising its hood—
The multi-headed cobra of passions!

The violent passions
The sannyasi had feared most,
He had known,
And deeply experienced,
They could throw him
Off his feet—
And could him or anyone
Mercilessly roast!

He wished to be one
Who had clearly won,
Registered a definitive victory—
And not just thereof boast!

Though he stood on the banks,
Often he was drawn in the currents.
Something inside cherished passions,
Just as loved guests are, by a host!

The sannyasi got further indrawn,
Getting deep in pure observation,
Silencing altogether the brain and the brawn
A point came when the culprit was caught
Entwined in the deepest roots of ego,
It was wrought.

He proceeded with utmost patience;

With the roots of the ego
Were uprooted the passions.

But then a miracle took place—
Simultaneously besides,
In the enlightenment he attained,
He rose to unimaginable heights,
Where all colours of life
Merged into the pure white of the Divine.
Saffron too was no longer a distinct shade
As he rose tall enough
To stay unaffected
By the passions' red!

Can we sing Life's song?

Can we sing life's song
When we hold ourselves as right
And all others as wrong?

Can we, O Lord,
Learn a few lessons from
The Nature's world
So immensely varied
And yet,
So beautifully adorned?

Such a varied world,
And yet,
Such a wonderful harmony!
Differences galore
Nature manifests
And spiritedly adore.

The vast, diverse world of vegetation—
An ocean of beauteous charm and sensation.

I wonder, why do we enter
A spirit so stark
As life sets out to evolve?
The fight for survival ensues, and,
Competition and conflicts throb!

Evolution doesn't mean
We can no longer learn
From the early stages
And their beautiful sight and scene!

Evolution doesn't mean
We need no longer be keen
To learn loyalty's lesson from a pigeon
And one in purity and love from a dove!

The world of wonderful creatures
Has endless wisdom to impart,

And so does the world of vegetation—
And its vast and complex treasure-trove!

As I reached out for a flower!

As I reached out for a flower
A thorn pierced through my palm.
Probably I was a little in haste!
Was I too offensive
For a flower too delicate?

Nature proceeds with so much caution
To create its family of flowers—
So beautiful, so fragile.
Does it stand in apprehension
Of our reckless hands
In name, human,
Yet often in nature vile?

A flower—its beauty, its fragrance—
To us humans is mostly a means
To offer at some altar
Of religion or ritual,
Or to satisfy some other whims!

A flower is a living entity too,
In itself it's a manifestation,
In its beauty, its fragrance,
And in the totality of Nature's scheme
They are meant to play a greater role
And by themselves they make a greater sense!

The diplomat spoke in measured tones!

The diplomat spoke in measured tones,
Every word he spoke
He weighed in ounce!

He posed like a seer
Who had mastered a global vision.
He knew when to possess
And when to renounce—
None for any spiritual cause,
But all for a material reason!

He seemed to have mastered practical wisdom,
From where flowed
His faculty of decision!

But the problem—the challenge— arose,
For he was a specimen of humanity too,
To represent which a complex chunk of theirs
chose
With a shrewd mind he manipulates other minds
Not that he never blends some colors of emotions
But he almost always falls short of
A must-to-master-and-muster humanity's dose!

Deep down in dejection!

Deep down in dejection,
When the vital force touches its base,
And the soul flutters to leave the bodily cage,
Disenchanted with the worldly race!

But the body is not just a vase,
That the soul descends in, lending its grace!
The body is not merely an apparel,
That the spirit puts on like a dress!

The body is a temple divine,
Through every cell of its case,
The divine doth sparkle and shine.
Through every pore of it,
The divine drinks and dine!

Let everything dark,
With its sombre song
Open out in the radiance of the Divine,
And learn how to sing
The celestial melodies of a skylark!

What is freedom if we don't grow!

What is freedom if we don't grow,
What is Growth if we don't grow in
Love and Compassion!

What is freedom if we don't grow
In some positive passion,
Which helps our higher energies unfold
And flows into our lives' crowning action!

Every life aspires for freedom,
In order it may manifest,
Its spirit's hidden light,
And its inmost beauty at its best!

But love and compassion
Are the ultimate test,
Failing which, it's a clear case,
We haven't touched our true depth
And our ultimate potential
Has yet got to unfold
And a big sign of interjection
Our lives have got to face!
Why to let the best of its potential
Remain unexplored
And the best of its energies
Allow to go waste!

Feeling through a thought!

Can you feel through a thought,
And think through a feeling?
Dig through the mindstuff
and carve a beautiful scene as you are tilling!

Have you seen a child
Making the world,
Look upside down
As it bends downwards
Takes a look from between her legs—
As it stands kneeling!

Sometimes emotions,
Under the stream of thoughts,
Sometimes the thoughts,
In the strong flow of emotions,
Are found reeling!

Either the child who knows
How to turn
The world upside down
Knows how to make
In between them a truce

Or, it's a seer,
Who pierces
through the nature
Of life and world, and,
Sees it through and through,
Can undertake the exercise
To fruitfully synthesize!

Turning our weakness into strength!

Yes, we can turn
Our weakness into strength,
As nature, in
Numerous nuances,
Doth prove and reflect!

Bamboo bends in storms
And does not break,
Being flexible isn't its weakness—
It's rather proven a strength!

A butterfly surely struggles a lot
To emerge free from its cocoon,
But that very struggle
Enables it to fly
And does its power enhance!

The lotus grows in muddy waters,
 Yet emerges as a beautiful flower
The very conditions that seem unfavorable
Actually do nourish it and strengthen!

A grain of sand enters
An oyster's shell,
It irritates the oyster.
But it refuses to suffer,
Instead it secretes
layers of nacre,
And transforms the irritant
Into a beautiful pearl.

The phoenix burns itself
To ashes, then rises anew, stronger than before.
Though a myth,
It symbolizes resilience—
how destruction or failure
Can lead to renewal
And greater strength!